THE DREAM *Journal*

DARE TO DREAM

BY PASTOR MATT HAGEE

First Printing January 2016
Second Printing April 2021

ISBN# 1-56908-029-1

CONTENTS

INTRODUCTION

Do We Dare to Dream?

No one ever enjoys the feeling of disappointment. The emotional weight makes it difficult to even breathe at times. We certainly will do our best to camouflage it. We smile and say, "It's no big deal." We brush it off with the statement "I totally understand." But no matter who you are, no matter where you encounter it, the truth is, no one likes to be disappointed.

Not only do we not like being disappointed, if you are like me, you don't like seeing others disappointed either. When I was a child, my parents would tell me that my eyeballs were like billboards and would advertise every emotion that I was feeling inside. Whether it was joy and delight or great disappointment, all anyone had to do was look me in the eyes to see exactly how I was feeling.

I can recall moments in my childhood when circumstances outside of my parents' control would interrupt our plans. Maybe dad had planned a fishing or hunting trip—two of my favorite things—and then a member of the church would pass away. Because of my dad's commitment to his role as pastor, he would have to reschedule our trip. I would say that I understood, but the weight of my disappointment was easy to see. Little did I know then how much it hurt him to see me disappointed. The only thing I could see from my perspective was we weren't going fishing when we planned to. It wasn't until years later, when I saw that same look in the eyes of my own children, that I understood how painful it is to disappoint someone you truly love.

It reminds me of what Jesus said in the Gospel of Matthew. Speaking to a crowd he said, "If you then, being evil, know how to give good gifts to your children, how much more will your Father who is in heaven give good things to those who ask Him!" (Matthew 7:11). He was reminding them that they, as earthly fathers, were far from perfect—yet they still desired to give their children the best they possibly could. Our Heavenly Father, in His perfection, is the same way. He desires to give us the very best.

Likewise, as much as we earthly fathers don't like to see our own children disappointed, our Heavenly Father loves us so much that He doesn't desire to see us disappointed either. The marvelous difference between God the Father and earthly fathers is God is in control. He's in control of all things great and small, and He made us this promise: all things, the pleasant and the unpleasant, the planned and the absolutely surprising, He will use them all for our good and for His glory if we are willing to remain faithful to His calling and purpose in our lives. The Apostle Paul affirmed this by saying, "And we know that all things work together for good to those who love God, to those who are the called according to His purpose" (Romans 8:28).

God loves when His children dare to dream because it shows great faith. When we trust in His promises more than the world around us, when we believe our heart's desire will come to pass rather than settling for less, when we dare to dream that God will fulfill His purposes in our lives, we are declaring to this world that our God is good and that our God is able.

This journal is for dreamers—those of you who are willing to write the vision down and make it plain so as to run the race with purpose. It is for those who have stopped dreaming—those of you who need to be reminded and encouraged that God didn't bring you this far to let you down. And this journal is for those of you who are too afraid to dream—who think that not dreaming today protects your heart from disappointment tomorrow.

In a world of hardships, God still has a wonderful plan for your life. He is not overwhelmed by the days in which we live, nor is He bothered by any predictions of difficulty that lie ahead. God is waiting to hear from His children, hoping we have enough boldness to ask Him to make our dream a reality.

Do we dare to dream? I say, with a God like our God, what do we have to lose?

SECTION 1

DARE TO DREAM

CHAPTER 1

A Season for Dreaming

Human beings are both blessed and burdened with short-term memory. Short-term memory allows us to more easily forget negative experiences so we more readily try again. However, the disadvantage is it also allows us to more easily forget foundational truths that help anchor our lives in seasons of uncertainty. For example, the prophet Isaiah reminds us that, "as the heavens are higher than the earth, so are My ways higher than your ways, and My thoughts than your thoughts" (Isaiah 55:9).

If we could remember this simple truth it would help us overcome so much anxiety and fear in our daily lives. If we trust in this world—the experts, the economic forecast, what our eyes can see—it would be very easy to convince ourselves that this is no time for dreaming. But if we look at what the Word of God says then we may well discover that this is our season to dream.

You may dream of starting a new business, owning a home, or investing in an opportunity that could be a blessing to you and others. What if now is the moment God has been waiting for, for you to take that next step of faith so that He can demonstrate, once again, that His ways are not our ways and His time is not our time?

GOD OUR PROVIDER

Don't let short-term memory loss cause you to forget what the Bible says about God's ability to provide. Think on these verses:

- *"And you shall remember the Lord your God, for it is He who gives you power to get wealth."*
  (Deuteronomy 8:18)

- *"'The silver is Mine, and the gold is Mine,' says the Lord of hosts."*
  (Haggai 2:8)

- *"And my God shall supply all your need according to His riches in glory by Christ Jesus."*
  (Philippians 4:19)

These three verses provide ample evidence that God is able to fund the resources of the dream that He has planted in your heart, even during the times when the financial experts say the risk is too great. Remember what Paul said, "If God is for us, who can be against us?" (Romans 8:31). But perhaps my favorite verse of all the financial promises found in the Word of God is 2 Corinthians 9:8: "And God is able to make all grace abound toward you, that you, always having all sufficiency in all things, may have an abundance for every good work."

Think of how much potential is in that one promise.

1) "GOD IS ABLE"

That one statement alone will revolutionize our existence if we will allow its truth to be planted in our hearts. No matter what you are facing, God is able.

When it comes to provision... God is able!

When it comes time to find that new job... God is able!

When others have to decide what to do without... God is able to sustain you!

When you are going to meet with the bank and need

favor... God is able!

When you are looking to set a record for sales or reach a new level of success within your company and all the doubters say there's just no way—that's when you need to be reminded that GOD IS ABLE!

2) "TO MAKE ALL GRACE ABOUND TOWARD YOU"

The key word in this statement is grace. If there is one thing we should be thankful for every single day, it's God's grace. His grace is what gives us what we don't deserve. We don't deserve forgiveness for our sin, but we've received it by His grace. We don't deserve the goodness and mercy of God, but He has made it available by His grace. We don't deserve salvation, but it is the gift of God given to us by His grace.

When it's time to dream, we need this reminder of grace. One of the first discouraging thoughts that crawls through our mind is what makes me think I deserve that? We have a natural tendency to place limitations on our lives based on a self-imposed sentence of guilt and condemnation.

You don't deserve good things—you haven't lived a perfect life... Thank God for grace!

You can't expect more, you're not worthy of what you have... Thank God for grace!

There's no earthly reason for you to believe that your dream will ever come true!... Thank God for grace!

If it wasn't for the amazing grace of God, none of us would be here today and there would be no reason to dream. But because God makes "all grace abound toward you," you have a Bible right to believe for great things in your life.

3) IT'S ABOUT YOU... "THAT YOU, ALWAYS HAVING ALL SUFFICIENCY IN ALL THINGS"

When it comes to our dreams and desires we often feel guilty if it's all about us. We've somehow convinced ourselves it's OK to want something good for other people, but it's selfish to desire anything good for our own lives. This is simply not true. It is not selfish to want something good in your own life. It's natural.

Look at it this way. When my four children sit down to eat dinner at my table each night they don't look at their food and refuse to eat it because their brother or sister may or may not like what is on their plate. If their sibling doesn't like the chicken that mom cooked for dinner, one of the kids is likely to say something like,

"Well if you're not going to eat that, you might as well pass it over here!" before they would ever consider joining those who are protesting the menu for the night.

It's the same way with God's children here on this earth. Just because some of His children choose not to enjoy the wonderful blessings He has made available to us all through His son Jesus Christ, doesn't mean you also are required to forfeit your blessings. You have His permission to believe for all that His Word has promised, and you can stand upon this promise while you do it. "You will have All Sufficiency in All Things..." He does not limit your life with what someone else is willing to believe or not believe. If God doesn't limit you, then you shouldn't either. If you're going to dream, dream big!

4) "THAT YOU MAY HAVE AN ABUNDANCE FOR EVERY GOOD WORK"

The fourth promise in this verse is that you would have abundance. By definition abundance is more than what is required. When God provides, it is not a "just enough" type of provision. When He is the one behind the work, it's a more than enough, abundant type of blessing. To me, one of the greatest indicators that the work I'm engaged in is God ordained is based on this thought: Is there abundance for the work? If the answer is yes, then I know that what I am engaged in is being blessed of God. If the answer is no, then I must reevaluate the project and consider if this is the right time to pursue it.

It will be the same with your dream. If it is the dream God has for your life, then there will be abundance because it is a good work, the kind of work He has promised in His Word to support. He may not give you the resources all at once, but He will be faithful to provide as you are faithful to believe and continue the work. What I am sure of—based upon His Word and personal experience—is that our God is able to provide.

A TIME TO DREAM

When it comes to dreaming you must consider the words of the prophet Joel: "And it shall come to pass afterward that I will pour out My spirit on all flesh; your sons and your daughters shall prophesy, your old men shall dream dreams, your young men shall see visions" (Joel 2:28). Understand that it does not matter whether you are awake and dreaming or asleep and dreaming. What matters is that it's a dream or vision given to you by God Almighty based on His Word and His Word alone.

Based on this verse, dreams and visions are something that occur when we have received the spirit of God in our lives. According to the scientific definition, a dream is an event that occurs in your subconscious during certain stages of sleep. Scientists say there is any number of reasons for this—from an overactive imagination to too much red sauce on your pizza or even what you watched last on television before you fell asleep. While there may be moments when this is true, according to what we find in this text, there are dreams and visions that are a result of God pouring out His spirit on us.

When is the right time to dream? If we keep reading in the book of Joel, the following verses are very specific about what is happening in the world around us during the exact time that God's spirit would be poured out.

> *"And I will show wonders in the heavens and in the earth: Blood and fire and pillars of smoke. The sun shall be turned into darkness, and moon into blood, before the coming of the great and awesome day of the Lord. And it shall come to pass that whoever calls on the name of the Lord shall be saved."*
> *(Joel 2:30–32)*

You don't have to search too far to find these exact things happening all around us today. Take for example the one statement about the moon being turned to blood. In 2014 and 2015 the world experienced a celestial phenomenon known in science as a tetrad—in layman's terms: "Four Blood Moons." Without getting too far into that topic, the fact that we are seeing those signs in the heavens is proof positive that God is saying to His children on earth: It's time for you to dream.

God wants to give you a glimpse of what He has in your future. He wants you to believe that He will provide the very best of things in the very worst of times. He wants you to remember that He is faithful to keep His promises even if the experts don't agree with His position. He certainly didn't require their permission to make the promise and He doesn't need their help bringing it to pass.

Do you dare to believe that there is a brighter day in your tomorrow? God wants you to. His grace, abundance, and favor are available to make your dream into a reality. All God is asking you to do is believe that He will do what He has said He will do, and then act like it. Watch Him do the rest. Remember that, "He who has begun a good work in you will complete it until the day of Jesus Christ" (Philippians 1:6).

SCRIPTURE TO REMEMBER

Matthew 7:11
Romans 8:28
Isaiah 55:9
Deuteronomy 8:18
Joel 2:28, 30–32
Haggai 2:8
Philippians 4:19
Romans 8:31
2 Corinthians 9:8
Philippians 1:6

THINGS TO DO

Think about what you consider your greatest dream to be. Write it down in plain and simple language that can be easily understood by anyone who reads it. For example: "I want to use my talent for the glory of God, to be a blessing to His Kingdom, to win the lost to Christ, and support my family."

As we continue through this journal, and as you continue to pray over the areas of your dream, you will be able to add more details to your dream as they become clearer. Right now, it is not as important for you to know every detail of your dream as much as it is important for you to believe God wants you to dream and to believe He can make your dream a reality.

What is your Greatest Dream?

What is your Greatest Dream? – continued

THINGS TO PRAY

Dreaming and praying go hand in hand. For one to come true you must be willing to engage faithfully in the other. People often wonder what they should pray. That's actually one of the many tricks of the enemy—to convince you that you don't know how to pray well enough so you give up before you ever begin. That's why I believe in praying the Word of God. You have a promise that it will not return void. So once you have written out your dream, write out the verses you want to pray over that dream and insert yourself in those words. For example:

"If God is for Matthew, then who can be against Matthew." (Romans 8:31)

"And God is able to make all grace abound toward Matthew, that I, always having all sufficiency in all things, may have an abundance for every good work." (2 Corinthians 9:8)

Once you have done this, simply read what you have written aloud, beginning with this opening prayer: "In the name of Jesus, based on the promise of Your Word, I declare that God is able to make all grace abound toward me when it comes to my dream. I can see my talents used for the glory of His Kingdom, and souls will be won to Christ because of it."

As we begin this journal, let's fulfill what the Word requires of us: to apply effort to our belief because faith without works is dead. Now get to work and let's start dreaming!

CHAPTER 2

WHAT IS A DREAM?

Now that we recognize this is a season to dream and that God wants us to dream, we need to define from a biblical perspective what a divine dream is and, more specifically, what a divine dream is not.

First let's identify what a divine dream is not. A divine dream will never contradict the written Word of God. Not for any reason should you ever allow anyone, anything, or any dream to cause you to violate the Word of God. Divine dreams do not contradict His Word—they prove His Word.

It would be difficult to adequately cover the topic of dreams from a biblical perspective without paying proper attention to the life of Joseph. He is the most famous example of a dreamer found in the Word of God. God revealed to Joseph a glimpse of his future, and Joseph had to be willing to endure extreme hardship and ridicule until the dream became a reality. But here is something you need to know about the dream that Joseph had and how it proved the Word of God.

Psalms 105:16–19 says, "Moreover [God] called for a famine in the land; He destroyed all the provisions of bread. He sent a man before them—Joseph—who was sold as a slave. They hurt his feet with fetters, he was laid in irons. Until the time that his word came to pass, the word of the Lord tested him."

In this passage, King David recalls what God has done, including the divine dream that God revealed to Joseph. Joseph had to endure a series of tremendous tests before he could see the plan of God fulfilled in His life. I will present more details about each of these tests later in the journal. However, it's important that you note from this example that the dream Joseph had didn't contradict the Word, it was fulfilled by it.

IT'S YOUR DREAM

The second thing you need to know about a dream is it will always be about you. Others may be in the dream but they are not the focus of it. Your dream is your dream and no one else's. If God wanted someone else to have it He would have given it to another person. This is important because sometimes we get discouraged when we decide to share our dream with someone else and they don't feel the same way we do about it. That's because that dream doesn't belong to anyone but you.

Look at it this way: when someone compliments my children I will agree with them and often join them in complimenting my kids.

"Pastor Matt, your son is so cute."

My response: "Thank you, and he's smart too!"

Now before you get upset with me for liking my kids, keep in mind I am not asking you to feel about them the way I do. They don't mean the same to you as they do to me. You can admire and enjoy them, but they are mine. Mine to live with, to raise, to train, to celebrate, to worry about, to pray over, and to take care of. It's exactly the same when it comes to your dream. It's all yours and no one else's. You can't be upset with someone else when he or she doesn't feel the same way you do about it. They weren't the ones entrusted with the dream like you were. It's yours to pray about, struggle with, endure and, in time, enjoy.

You need to recognize that the dream is about you because other people may appear in your dreams—again, this kind of dreaming can happen whether you're awake or asleep. It's like a cameo appearance from another actor in a movie. They just seem to show up. Even then the dream is not about them, it's about you. Other folks appear in your dream because they represent or symbolize something you are learning.

For example, I have heard single people say they are dreaming about a married person. I must warn you: its dangerous territory to lay claim to something or someone you have no business even thinking about. However, when you put your dream in the right context, you understand that a single person often has a natural, God-given desire to be in a marriage relationship.

Now, let's put the rules to the formula to work and see if it provides insight.

1) THE DIVINE DREAM WILL NEVER CONTRADICT THE WORD OF GOD.

The Word of God says, "What God has joined together, let no man put asunder" so He would never give a single person a dream that would ruin another person's marriage or life.

2) THE DREAM IS ABOUT YOU.

If you happen to see a married couple in your dream, it could very well be that they represent what God wants you to begin believing for—a marriage like they have. No, not specifically their marriage, but a marriage that is honoring and wholesome. It could very well be God's way of letting you know that when you do what they have done, you too can have what they have. Remember, He is no respecter of persons.

With this in mind let's continue to define a divine dream from a biblical perspective.

JACOB THE DREAMER

Remember Jacob's dream? "Then he dreamed, and behold, a ladder was set up on the earth, and its top reached to heaven; and there the angels of God were ascending and descending on it" (Genesis 28:12).

We know from our rules that the dream is about Jacob. Jacob's dream was God's way of revealing the nature of the relationship that God wanted to have with Jacob. All of Jacob's life he attempted to gain the favor of his earthly father Isaac but, as you know from the biblical account, Isaac favored Esau. The war between the brothers began even in the womb when Rebekah said she could feel the children wrestling within her. On the day the boys were born Esau arrived first and Jacob was a close second as he came out of his mother's womb holding his brother's heel.

The struggle didn't end there. Jacob later bargained with a bowl of beans for Esau's birthright. Esau valued the temporary things, and Jacob wanted what could not be bought—the favor of his father. Then when Isaac was close to death and lying blind on his bed, Jacob deceived Isaac by disguising himself as Esau in order to receive his father's blessings. This trickery caused such a family feud that Jacob had to run for his life. While on the run, God gave him a divine dream; it was a glimpse of what Jacob could have in his life.

God let him know in the next few verses:

> *"I am the Lord God of Abraham your father and the God of Isaac; the land on which you lie I will give to you and your descendants. Also your descendants shall be as the dust of the earth; you shall spread abroad to the west and the east, to the north and the south; and in you and in your seed all the families of the earth shall be blessed. Behold, I am with you and will keep you wherever you go, and will bring*

> *you back to this land; for I will not leave you until I have done what I have spoken to you." (Genesis 28:13–15)*

The Word of God proved the dream; it did not contradict it. Even before the history of the descendants of Jacob was recorded, God said in a divine dream, "I will be with you and I will bring you back to this land." The children of Israel came to that land for the first time with Joshua after they left the wilderness. Then they came back to that land with Nehemiah after the exile and captivity of Babylon. Finally, they returned to their land a third time in 1948, following the horror of the Holocaust. What God gave Jacob in a dream has been proven even by current morning headlines! God is still with Israel and Israel is still in their land promised to them by God Himself.

JOSEPH THE DREAMER

Remember Joseph's dream? "Now Joseph had a dream, and he told it to his brothers; and they hated him even more" (Genesis 37:5).

What brought such a strong response? Joseph, who was already greatly disliked because he was "daddy's boy," now informs his brothers that he dreamed they were all going to bow before him and he was going to be exalted above them. I can't imagine why they didn't shout for joy and ask him to share his story over and over again.

As a matter of fact, it made them so angry that a few verses later they actually said, "'Look this dreamer is coming! Come therefore, let us now kill him and cast him into some pit.... We shall see what will become of his dreams!'" (Genesis 37:19–20).

Remember the rules? The dream is always about you. Others may appear in your dream, but the main character is always you. You must be willing to endure and pursue what God has in store for your life. The reason that Joseph's brothers appeared in his dream was both literal and symbolic. The literal reason was they would indeed one day bow before Joseph as he sat on the throne in Egypt. The symbolic reason was that, by God's sovereign hand exalting Joseph at the right time, in the right place, and giving him divine insight, he, Joseph, would save the world.

You may read the story and conclude, "Well I only see how he saved Egypt and the sons of Jacob." Consider what would have happened if those sons had not been saved. There would be no Israel, there would be no Judah, there would be no David, there would be no Jesus and the world would indeed be lost. Isn't it amazing to see how lives are changed when someone has the courage to believe in and live out their dream?

THE COST OF A DREAM

A dream is a divine glimpse of what God has in your future. It is about you, and it will never contradict God's Word but fulfill it. Have you ever considered how much dreamers must endure to see their dreams become reality? Just because Jacob and Joseph had dreams doesn't mean God handed them a free ride down easy street. They both faced a series of very real challenges which they willingly chose to overcome with resolve and faith in God in order to see the dream come true. For the sake of time, we will finish this chapter considering the challenges of Joseph, although Jacob had his fair share of challenges too.

CHALLENGE #1: DON'T TRANSFORM, CONFORM

When Joseph's brothers heard about his dream, they mocked him, despised him, and wanted him to lose faith in his dream immediately. Why? Because they were threatened by the fact his dream made him different and gave him a purpose, a higher calling. They couldn't stand it. They wanted him to accept the fact that he was just one of Jacob's boys, born to tend the flock and nothing more. But rather than be conformed to their limitations, Joseph was willing to believe what God revealed to him—even when he was standing in the bottom of a dark pit listening to his own brothers mock him, curse him, and plan his demise.

There are times when you will have to remind yourself that the divine dream God gave you was for you, and that if God is for you no one can stand against you. You cannot base your progress on the actions or beliefs of others—especially when others would prefer you remain like everyone else rather than believe God has something more for your life. However, if God has shown you more, then believe for more because all things are possible to those who believe!

CHALLENGE #2: DISAPPOINTMENT

Can you imagine how disappointed Joseph was when he found himself sold into slavery? This is not what he dreamed about! This was not the path to being exalted, or was it? As human beings, we do not see things as God sees them. We cannot tell a good day from a bad one. He is the one who sees the end from the beginning and He has simply asked us to trust Him and believe that His plan will come to pass.

Joseph didn't give up on his dream even as he was sold into slavery. He applied himself; he went to work as if everything in Potiphar's house belonged to him. He wasn't scrubbing Potiphar's floor—he scrubbed the floor under his command. Potiphar was so impressed with Joseph's work ethic and responsibility that he promoted Joseph to overseer of his entire estate. Yet even as overseer of the estate, Joseph wasn't where he wanted to be. Once again, he didn't give in to disappointment. He instead continued to gain favor and experience that would serve him well later in life when his dream did come true.

I know a number of people who have forfeited their divine dream because of disappointment. The road was much harder and rockier, and contained far more twists and turns than they anticipated, so they abandoned the dream rather than to continue believing what God revealed. Before Joseph could rule over Egypt he had to learn to rule over himself. Sometimes the best place for this kind of training is not in a position of comfort, but struggle. Struggle is where you gain strength and strength helps you endure until the dream comes true. When you are faced with less than you expected, don't quit! Keep going and see what happens when you endure to the end.

CHALLENGE #3: TEMPTATION

"So it was, as she spoke to Joseph day by day, that he did not heed her, to lie with her or to be with her" Genesis 39:10. Sometimes the thing that will kill your dream is a lack of character. Dreamers must be people with character as well as strength. We all know Potiphar's wife had an eye for Joseph, but this verse gives some insight into how he felt about her. It says she spoke to him "day by day." If this wasn't a matter of temptation for Joseph we wouldn't have heard about it. Because it was something he struggled with, we get to learn from his experience and see how this test moved him further on the path toward fulfilling his dream.

First consider this: If Joseph wasn't tempted by the opportunity to be with Potiphar's wife then why did he offer her an explanation about his refusal to engage in this behavior, "My master has entrusted everything in house to me but you..." Just think for a moment on how the gnawing nature of temptation wears on the soul. It is one thing to say "no" once, but "day by day"! With each sultry invitation, the justifications to give in are running through Joseph's head, "I am not in my father's house; I'm in Egypt, and as they say, 'What happens in Egypt stays in Egypt.'" Who knows how many logical, circumstantial, and carnal excuses he could have used to justify why he should not be judged too strongly for giving in. However, Joseph gets to the heart of the matter in one statement: "How then can I do this great wickedness, and sin against God?" (Genesis 39:9).

Think of the personal conviction and faith that is demonstrated with these words. Joseph didn't say, "I don't want to" he said, "If I did, it would be a sin against the one who created me." So many times we seem to ask the wrong question when it comes to sin. We like to ask, "Will God forgive me?" The answer is of course He will. "Will God still love me?" He will without a doubt, forever and always. But the really hard question to ask when it comes to the sin in our lives is not "does God love us?" but "do we love God enough not to sin?" The choice in the matter isn't His but ours.

Joseph didn't share these words during a season of amazing miracles and great outpourings of God's presence. He was a slave in a foreign land. If there was a time for him to say, "Well, God hasn't shown up lately, guess I get to walk on the wild side," this would have been it! I know the logic sounds weak, but I have heard this type of reasoning more times than I would like to count in the years that I've been a pastor. However, in spite of all that Joseph could have done he simply said "No" again and again, until the temptress became vengeful and decided to accuse him of the very thing he had repeatedly resisted.

CHALLENGE #4: LEARNING HOW TO ENDURE

For all of Joseph's hard work and effort he received a one-way ticket to the darkest dungeon in Egypt. How wonderful, right? Actually, when you consider the biblical text it's almost as if Potiphar took Joseph's side. For one thing, as a slave, Joseph was his master's property. If Potiphar thought he was guilty of such a violation he could have had him killed on the spot and no one would have thought twice about a guilty slave executed for his crimes. Also, Potiphar placed Joseph in the King's prison, "a place where the king's prisoners were confined" (Genesis 39:20). It was as if the general pulled some strings to make sure Joseph was treated as well as could be expected considering the circumstance.

Finally, take a look at the situation from heaven's perspective. If Potiphar's wife doesn't falsely accuse Joseph, then Potiphar would have never considered getting rid of Joseph. Everything that Joseph touched was blessed. If Joseph remained in Potiphar's house, how would Pharaoh ever come to know him? This connection occurred because Joseph was held in the same location as the King's prisoners. From our natural perspective, Joseph's dream just took a major step backwards. From heaven's point of view "The Dreamer" just took a giant step forward. Now all that's left for Joseph to do is not give up, and to keep on believing that his divine dream was still going to come to pass.

While in prison, Joseph met two of the king's prisoners who were tormented by their dreams. Joseph had compassion on them both. "Why do you look so sad?" he asked (Genesis 40:7). It didn't matter what he had gone through personally, he still took the time to care for others. Sometimes the fastest way to make your dream come true is to help someone else with theirs.

Not only did Joseph demonstrate compassion for others, he lets us know that he himself had not lost faith. The men told Joseph they had had dreams, but there was no one to give an interpretation. Joseph said, "'Do not interpretations belong to God? Tell them to me, please'" (Genesis 40:8). Even though his own dreams had not yet come to pass, Joseph still believed that God was the one who could provide him with the meaning of dreams, and he was willing to help these men understand theirs. Joseph chose to be a blessing and comfort to others even as he endured the stress of prison life.

CHALLENGE #5: PROMOTION

Sometimes the hardest thing to overcome is success. I have seen people struggle for years to achieve a goal only to fall apart the moment they achieve it. I have heard it said that talent will take you to the top, but discipline will keep you on top. Joseph finally finds himself before Pharaoh and is appointed as the operational manager for the entire kingdom. Joseph demonstrates great discipline in not seeking vengeance on all those who had wronged him along the way. He didn't spend his first thirty days in office letting Potiphar carry out his trash and shine his shoes. He understood there was a divine purpose to it all. He could no more take vengeance than he could lay blame because only God could have caused all of these things to happen as they did.

CHALLENGE #6: FORGIVENESS

The last struggle Joseph had to contend with in the biblical story was the reconciliation of his family. He had made it through what some would call the hardest part: moving from the pit to the palace. But what do you do when those who hurt you most are standing in front of you and you have the power to take revenge? You forgive them. You speak words of grace and remember what was said throughout the story of Joseph: "And the Lord was with Joseph." No matter who put Joseph where, God was with him. In the pit, in temptation, in prison—God never left His side, and He will never leave yours.

Are you starting to see the costs associated with receiving a God-given divine dream? There are no shortcuts. But the end result will be greater than you can ever imagine if you are willing to endure the struggles until the dream comes to pass.

SCRIPTURE TO REMEMBER

Psalms 105:16–19
Genesis 28:12, 13–15
Genesis 37, 39–43

THINGS TO DO

Write down the struggles that you are facing at this moment and those you have endured. Is there any past action you need to make right? If so, be sure to do it because those broken pieces of your past may be the very thing that enables you to move closer to your divine dream.

What struggles are you facing?

What struggles have you endured?

ARE THERE PAST ACTIONS YOU SHOULD MAKE RIGHT?

THINGS TO PRAY

Consider what you have written down and what you are struggling with. Take the time to assign scripture to each of these areas and pray over them until you break through and can say, by God's grace, that you overcame. Remember, just as God was with Joseph, He's also with you—and if God is for you who can be against you!

SECTION 2

DREAM KILLERS

CHAPTER 3

Dream Killer #1: Impatience

As we explore further what it means to be a dreamer, we turn to the interim period between when you first recognize your dream and when it is fulfilled. You need to know there are a lot of ways you can destroy your dream during this season. The next seven chapters will cover the seven Dream Killers—attitudes and actions that can thwart the very dream we long to see fulfilled—and how to guard against them to ensure your dream becomes a reality.

We live in a society where we want everything and we want it now! As a matter of fact, all you have to do these days to sell something is use the word "faster." This computer downloads faster; this phone is faster; this oven bakes cookies, and pies, and turkeys faster. We're always in a hurry, and much of the time we really don't know why.

It's OK to seek out faster technology, or even a faster way of cooking, but when it comes to our divine destiny we need to know it takes time. God does not give us a guided tour of the rest of our lives in one brief dream. He reveals a little at a time—sometimes He shows us what's just ahead, and sometimes He reveals the final outcome without showing us how we are going to get there.

I believe Paul was dead-on when he wrote, "Oh, the depth of the riches both of the wisdom and knowledge of God! How unsearchable are His judgments and His ways past finding out!" (Romans 11:33). It may be pure poetry, but it is also a strong reminder that trying to understand why God does what He does the way He does it is a futile exercise for the limited mind of man.

GOD'S TIMING ISN'T OUR TIMING

Psalms 27:14 gives us clear instruction on the ways of a dreamer: "Wait on the Lord; be of good courage, and He shall strengthen your heart." Though counterintuitive, a dreamer does a lot of waiting. But waiting is not a natural habit of ours. When God gives us a glimpse of what is to come we want to race to the end immediately to receive the promise rather than to allow God to get us there in His time. We often grow impatient. We begin to take matters into our own hands. And that's when we really make things difficult for ourselves.

Maybe God revealed to you that you will enjoy future business success. So you immediately go out and buy all of the material things you wish to own even before success arrives. Think of it as counting your chickens before they hatch. Sadly, there are some who do this very thing—or something even more foolish—and then believe God is going to show up and pay for all the checks that can't be cashed. Folks, that's not the way faith works, and that's not what your divine dream should inspire you to do.

Remember: "we walk by faith" (2 Corinthians 5:7). By that very definition faith happens one step at a time. So when you are given a dream, make sure you walk it out by faith. Don't be tempted to jump ahead to see if you can speed things up. That never works. God is the God of today, yesterday, and tomorrow. He is not only taking care of you right now, He is also preparing your future so that when you and your future arrive at the same place everything is as it should be. Exodus 23:20 says, "Behold, I send an Angel before you to keep you in the way and to bring you into the place which I have prepared." God has us right where He wants us and we have no business arriving ahead of schedule.

Now if we attempt to get ahead of Him then we become like the people the Prophet Isaiah was speaking to, "Your ears shall hear a word from behind you saying, 'This is the way walk in it'" (30:21). Consider this for a moment: If we are the sheep of God's pastures, and we are following our Good Shepherd, are we supposed to be in front of the Shepherd? Of course not! So why would the voice we hear come from behind us unless we were out of position? The point is we were never supposed to get out in front of the Shepherd—our place is behind the Good Shepherd, following His lead through "the paths of righteousness" as found in Psalms 23:3. If we get impatient, if we get out in front of the Shepherd, we are going to kill our dream because we will either arrive too soon or run right past it.

A LAMP UNTO MY FEET

I personally like the description in Psalms 119:105: "Your word is a lamp unto my feet and a light to my path." This verse paints the picture of an ancient oil lamp, not a five-million-candle spotlight. It is a lamp that only gave enough light for someone to see what was directly in front of them—taking one cautious step at a time. The light that emanated from this lamp could not reveal what was at the end of the road, only what was directly in front of the one carrying it.

Now certainly there will be seasons in your life where you will be able to move faster because it's familiar ground and you know the way. However, there will also be those steep and jagged places where each move could make the difference between success or failure. It is during those times that you must take hold of the lamp of God's Word and let it light the path before you so you can take your next step with confidence.

As you make progress toward your dream step-by-step, whatever you do, don't allow yourself to grow weary in well doing. It is not unusual to experience frustration as we wait on God for our dream to come to pass. Sometimes we may decide to quit all together. But Galatians 6:9 exhorts us to: "not grow weary while doing good, for in due season we shall reap if we do not lose heart." There is a season designated by the King of Kings when your dream is due. Your job is to be patient and wait upon the Lord who promises to turn your dream into reality.

SCRIPTURE TO REMEMBER

Romans 11:33
Psalm 27:14
2 Corinthians 5:7
Galatians 6:9
Exodus 23:20
Isaiah 30:21
Psalms 119:105

THINGS TO DO

Consider on whose efforts you are depending. Are you striving to achieve your dream your way? Or, by waiting on the Lord, are you allowing Him to guide your every step? In the context of your dream, consider whether you are at peace right now or whether you are anxious and worried because something is out of place. Write down what you wish were different in the space below and ask yourself if this concern is driven by internal factors like impatience, or external factors like someone else's preferences for your life. No matter the answer, begin to apply the scriptures above to the areas of concern until you are at peace.

What do you wish was different?

Are these concerns driven by internal or external factors?

THINGS TO PRAY

If you are struggling with impatience, pray the Word of God over yourself. Pray that the peace of God would rule your heart and mind in Christ Jesus. Pray that you will walk by faith and not by sight. Ask God to show you your next step by the lamp of His Word. And pray daily to believe and rest in the truth that God's ways are not your ways.

CHAPTER 4

DREAM KILLER #2: REFUSAL TO LISTEN TO GODLY COUNSEL

"The way of a fool is right in his own eyes,
but he who heeds counsel is wise."
—Proverbs 12:15

One of the greatest problems we face in our culture today is our unwillingness to be teachable. Jesus calls us to be disciples. As a matter of fact, those who followed Jesus Christ called Him "teacher." Why? Because Jesus was training them to be like Him. Here's a little experiment I challenge you to try: The next time you're having a conversation with someone, count the number of times you hear the phrase "I know," whether said by you or by the other person. It is an attitude ingrained in our day and age. "I know this..." and "I know that..." and "I know, right... ?" Oh and don't forget: "You know..." It's everywhere! This lack of a teachable spirit can wreak havoc when it comes to our dreams. If we want to see our dream come to fruition, we must admit we don't know everything, and we must be willing to accept Godly counsel from those who have walked a similar path before us.

If your dream is to own a successful business, then you must be willing to receive counsel from other successful businessmen. Because they have already faced the giants you're about to fight and climbed the mountains you're about climb, why not take the time to hear what they have to say?

Do you want a successful marriage? Visit with someone who has been married to the same person for 40, 50, or 60 years. Don't listen to those who spend their time complaining about their spouse or their marriage. Instead, seek out those who are involved in a successful marriage, ask them how they achieved and maintain it and then be willing to apply what they share.

LISTENING REQUIRES HUMILITY

It has always been my dream to be the Pastor of Cornerstone Church. I actually cannot remember a day when I didn't truly want to be the pastor of our Church.

Sure, when I told others about my dream as a child they would pat me on the head and say, "You're so cute, you want to be just like your daddy!" But it was much deeper than that. It was truly the desire of my heart, and I believe it was the divine dream God placed inside me.

I began working in the church at the age of twelve in the children's ministry. I was involved in youth group, setting up and tearing down the equipment and even worked the ministry product tables at events across the country. I participated as often as possible, from my teenage years all the way through college. But there was one afternoon in my father's study when all of that training could have come to an abrupt end.

I was seventeen years old and had just graduated from high school. Since ORU classes began the first week of August, my father planned for me to preach the last Sunday night of July. In the moment, I didn't understand his strategy behind that timing, but as I look back now I recognize my father had a plan: he timed my preaching as close to my departure date as possible so if anyone came looking for me after that service he could simply state, "He's gone out of town and cannot be reached!" Needless to say, my dad is a man of great wisdom and had experience on his side.

I was so excited to preach I could hardly stand

it. I studied, I read, I found old theology books that had words I didn't even understand—and the bigger the word the better it sounded! I watched Christian television. I paid attention to how all of my favorite speakers changed the tone of their voices, how they got louder and softer, how they prowled around the platform. After almost two months of preparation and forty-three pages of notes, I was ready! I was ready to raise the roof and let heaven in! I knew this was going to be the beginning of another great awakening, and the members of our congregation, including my own family members, were going to swoon under the power of what I had to say. I mean this was my moment! I knew what I wanted to do! I knew what I wanted to say! I knew... I knew... I knew... NOTHING!

One afternoon my father called and said, "Matt, I'm going to be home at four this afternoon and I'd like to look over your sermon notes." I was so excited to hand him the Magna Carta of my ministry. I was thrilled for him to hold the firstborn child of my pastoral genius in his hands. With a confident stride I walked into his study, handed him my pile of notes, and began to wait. It didn't take long. Within three lines he asked me to get him his red pen. I wondered why he would need that for such a work of perfection. Surely it was for a punctuation error.

Not hardly.

For the next forty-five minutes he crossed out, circled, scribbled through, and wrote notes in the margin. Then he would throw page after page on the floor. It was painful to watch. It looked like he had killed a small animal on each and every page and then sent them twirling to the ground like a collapsed parachute. After the blood bath, he took two pages of the original document, looked me in the eyes, and said words that are seared in my memory and written on my soul to this day: "On these two pages are words that came from the Bible. Everything on the floor came from you. If you preach what you believe, people will not cross the street to hear it. But if you preach the Word, they will come from all over the world to hear it."

Those words hold enough truth to fill a seminary, but did they bless me at the time? Nope. I was mad and offended. How dare he not understand my genius! Why wasn't he willing to let me be me? Who did he think he was?

As absurd as it sounds, these were my exact thoughts.

I slowly gathered up all of my forsaken notes as if they were orphaned children, and I carried them back to my study. I slammed the door behind me loud enough to let the whole house know I was upset... but not loud enough to be rebellious. There is always a fine line you know.

There I sat mentally building my case. I began preparing my argument and getting ready for round two. Then suddenly, I heard that still small voice. It was the one Elisha describes in 1 Kings 19:12 and it asked me a question: "Is this where it ends?" I sat there a very long time trying to make sense of the question. I knew it was the Holy Spirit talking to me—I had heard Him before—but how could this be the end of my ministry? I hadn't even preached my first sermon yet! How could my dream be over before it ever began? It was because I was unwilling to listen to Godly counsel and advice.

The longer I thought about the question, the more I started to see the faces of other pastors I had met over the years at different conferences, events, and services. I remembered how they would come up to me and say, "I wish I could just sit for an hour and talk to your dad.... If I could have one day of his time to ask him questions.... I need some advice about my church and I know he would have the answer." Here I was just a few feet away from what so many around the country wanted access to. And rather than listening to him and learning from him, in my ignorance and pride I was going to argue with him. Wow, how foolish!

God knew what my dream was. He's the one who gave it to me. He knew that in order for my dream to become a reality I would need to be trained, and He placed me in the perfect place to be trained: at my father's feet. God orchestrated it all and I was about to throw it away because I didn't want to listen to Godly counsel.

So, instead of heading back to my father's study for round two, I grabbed an empty legal pad and a pen, took the Bible, went back to his room and said, "Dad, if you will show me how to do this, then that's the way I will do it from now on."

In that moment, all I had to do to make the dream come true was listen and learn. And in that moment, all I had to do to kill the dream was refuse the Godly council of a wise and experienced pastor. Humble yourself and understand that God has you right where you need to be in order to learn what you need to know to accomplish your divine dream.

SCRIPTURE TO REMEMBER

Proverbs 12:15

THINGS TO DO

Consider your dream and then make a list of Godly people who possess wisdom and experience in that area. Reach out to them and ask if they would be willing to mentor you. Offer to be of service to them in a context where you will learn from them—the fastest way to learn is to do!

List Godly people who possess wisdom and experience where your dream is concerned

THINGS TO PRAY

Ask the Lord to give you a teachable spirit. Anytime you feel pride beginning to take over, stop what you're doing and pray for the strength to die to self and to press on.

CHAPTER 5

Dream Killer #3: Being Persuaded by Ungodly People

The Apostle Paul posed this question to the New Testament church and it is worth asking again as you consider your divine dream: "What does light have to do with darkness?" (see 2 Corinthians 6:14). Just as not taking Godly advice can kill your dream, allowing ungodly people to persuade you to believe and act in ungodly ways will guarantee your dream's destruction. Remember it was God Almighty who gave you your dream. It is a glimpse into your divine destiny. If God gave it to you then He will be the One who makes it possible for your dreams to come true. However, when you turn to ungodly counsel you forfeit the opportunity to experience the great and mighty things God has purposed for you.

Now let me be clear: There is nothing wrong with asking for guidance from people who have the knowledge and expertise needed to achieve a goal. But there is a difference between guidance and persuasion. Guidance is counsel or advice while persuasion is inducing someone to follow a belief system. That is why you should not allow yourself to be persuaded by ungodly people—because it changes your beliefs. You will know you are under someone's persuasion when you begin to allow their behavior to change yours. You start to act like he acts, talk like she talks, think like he thinks, and you do it because you believe he or she has the answers to the questions you face. Think of the disciples. They were under the persuasion of Jesus Christ. He taught them the principles of the Kingdom and they began to behave so much like Him that they would later be known as Christians or "Little Christ's." Persuasion makes us little disciples of those we follow.

PERSUASION IS PROGRESSIVE

One of the most distressing problems the church faces today is when a believer proclaims one thing but behaves in an entirely different manner. This dilemma is not a new one and it is very dangerous for the body of Christ. King David even addressed this issue in Psalm 1:1: "Blessed is the man, who walks not in the counsel of the ungodly, nor stands in the path of sinners, nor sits in the seat of the scornful."

In this verse David points out the progressive nature of ungodly persuasion. You begin by walking, then standing, and finally sitting. These actions may seem similar in nature but when you consider their full meaning you discover the depth of what David is saying. Step one is walking. In order to receive "counsel" while walking, you must be going in the same direction as the one giving the counsel. You may not be fully committed to the person by your side but you understand a bit more about their life choices. There may even be certain things about them or their beliefs you are now willing to accept.

Step two is standing. The ungodly counselor has your attention now. You have stopped moving forward and are now listening intently to their persuasive rhetoric. You may even take a stand on their behalf. You begin to represent their cause and defend their position.

Step three is sitting. You are not going anywhere. You have chosen to sit and fellowship among the ungodly—to become who they are and to distance yourself from foundational truths because your beliefs have changed and you see things in a whole new way.

We are experiencing this phenomenon more and more in our world of relative truth. We are willing to listen to ungodly counsel, reasoning in our minds that it must be acceptable. It must be acceptable to change the definition of marriage, to murder an unborn child in his or her mother's womb, or to believe there is more than one way to God in heaven. I know there are many of you reading this and thinking that's a bit of a stretch, but you would be very alarmed to know how many Christians defend these positions daily. You may ask, "How did they ever begin thinking this way?" Easy, they began by walking, then standing, and finally sitting among the persuasive ungodly.

UNGODLY PERSUASION IN JOSEPH'S LIFE

Consider Joseph and the ungodly persuasion he endured from those around him. First his rebellious brothers tried to persuade him to also rebel against their father. One of the ways the ungodly persuade others is through peer pressure. If it is acceptable to the majority, why would you want to be the odd man out?

Then there was the ungodly persuasion of Potiphar's wife, repeatedly tempting Joseph to engage in a sexual relationship and compromise his personal values for her own carnal desire. Don't ever forget this fact when the ungodly attempt to persuade you—it's not you they are looking out for! They only want to use you for their own gratification.

If Joseph had caved to the ungodly persuasion around him, he would have killed his dream long before God ever brought it to fruition. As you walk faithfully in the direction of your divine dream, remain steadfast like Joseph. As essential as it is to receive the counsel of the Godly, you must also be certain you rebuke the persuasion of the ungodly. It is a dream killer! In order for your divine dream to become a reality you must remember God is the One who gave you the dream and He is the One who called you to your divine destiny. It is God and God alone who will be faithful in causing your dream to become a reality—only remain steadfast in Him.

SCRIPTURE TO REMEMBER

2 Corinthians 6:14
Psalms 1:1–6

THINGS TO DO

Consider areas in your life that are being pursued

by ungodly people or unholy principles and make note of them. Commit to walk away from them. Search for a scripture verse that applies to the area you are struggling with and write it down. Earnestly pray that scripture over the situation on a daily basis until the stronghold is broken.

WHAT AREAS IN YOUR LIFE ARE BEING PURSUED BY UNGODLY PEOPLE OR UNHOLY PRINCIPLES?

List scriptures that apply to the areas in your life previously mentioned.

THINGS TO PRAY

Ask God to show you if you are walking, standing, or sitting amid ungodly counsel. As God reveals areas to you, go to the Word to find His truth. Write those Scriptures and memorize them. Pray for God to ground you in His ways so you may prosper in whatever you do.

CHAPTER 6

Dream Killer #4: Doubt

Have you ever made a decision and then later doubted if it was the right thing to do? Maybe you sold your home only to look back and dearly wish you could undo it. Maybe a relationship ended and now you doubt you'll ever find someone better. Or maybe you look in the mirror and doubt you have what it takes to be a good spouse or to build your own business. A word of warning: doubt can destroy your dream before it ever begins. If you want to destroy the dream God gave you, all you have to learn to say is, "I doubt that."

God wants to give you blessings!

"I doubt that."

God wants to do great things in your life!

"I doubt that."

God wants to turn your very big dream into your very big reality!

"I doubt that."

Listen to what the Bible says about doubt. The book of James tells us to, "ask in faith, with no doubting, for he who doubts is like a wave of the sea driven and tossed by the wind. For let not that man suppose that he will receive anything from the Lord..." (James 1:6–7).

Why is doubt so destructive? Because when we doubt, our focus, our energy, our confidence, and our momentum falter. James describes someone who doubts as "double-minded and unstable in every way" (James 1:8). A person who doubts is literally undecided between truth and untruth. When we doubt, we allow our imagination to play with a lie rather than to believe what is good and true. And in that moment of undecidedness, the wind drives and tosses us from a foundation of truth until we're lost in a sea of despair. When we are finally able to look up again, suddenly our dream is nowhere in sight.

IT'S A CHOICE

But there is good news! Doubt is a learned behavior. Doubt is a choice. We can just as easily choose to believe as we can choose to doubt. In fact, choosing to believe is actually easier because we can stand on the unmoving Word of God.

When doubt enters your mind you have a choice—keep that thought and let it take root in your mind and heart, or speak the Word of God to yourself. You can say, "I doubt that." Or you can remind yourself that God's ways are not your ways. This journey toward your dream may not look like what you imagined, but God isn't finished yet!

There are also times when doubt doesn't come from within us; sometimes it comes from those around us. If you are surrounded by people who say your dream won't come true, you don't need a new dream—what you need are new friends! Why? Because doubters are a demolition crew to the divine destiny placed in your life. Don't allow others to tear down what God Himself will build. When the whole world says that your dream will never come to pass, keep believing in that dream.

Take every doubt captive before it takes you captive. God will honor your dream as long as you don't allow doubt to interfere.

SCRIPTURE TO REMEMBER

James 1:6–8

THINGS TO DO

Do you have doubts about your dream? If so, write those down and determine what Scripture you can memorize to combat those doubts. Consider, too, if there are any people in your life who cause you to doubt your dream. Then pray about that relationship and how you should move forward with it.

List any doubts you have about your dream

WHAT SCRIPTURES CAN COMBAT THESE DOUBTS?

List the people in your life that cause you to doubt your dream and pray for those relationships

THINGS TO PRAY

Ask the Lord to show you any places of doubt. Ask Him to help you take these thoughts captive and replace them with truth from His Word. Ask God to make you “stable in every way.”

CHAPTER 7

Dream Killer #5: Avoiding Struggle

We do ourselves a disservice when we believe struggle only happens to people who bring it on themselves. Struggle happens to everyone. I've never met a pregnant woman who enjoys labor, but labor is what brings our precious children into this world. If a woman were to forfeit the struggle of labor, what would happen to that child? What if instead of being a bad thing, struggle is actually the mechanism that propels our dream into a reality? What if struggle is our own version of giving birth to our dream?

The fifth way to destroy your dream is to quit at the first sign of trouble. We too often fall into this trap of believing that because we've got a divine dream that our path toward its fulfillment will be easy. We get a vision of God's future for our life and take off with power, purpose, and enthusiasm. We begin to walk out

God's plan and then something happens that causes struggle. It gets hard, we quickly forfeit, and we give up on that God-given dream.

Some of us even use struggle as a marker of divine guidance. We suddenly get spiritual and say things like "Well, this must not be the will of God—otherwise it wouldn't be this hard." Or, "God must not be for this dream because there are people working against it." Listen, if the power of hell isn't fighting against you, it's walking with you.

Here's what the Bible has to say about struggle: "Many are the afflictions of the righteous, but the Lord delivers him out of them all" (Psalm 34:19). Trouble isn't a sign that we're failing. Most of the time, struggle is a sign that we're getting ready for a breakthrough. Rejoice and be exceedingly glad if you're in a day of trouble, because God is cheering you on! And as long as God is for you, who can be against you?

Struggle Has Purpose

The bottom line is nobody likes struggle. But struggle is not without purpose. If you come up against struggle, recognize that it's a preview for the victory party when you declare yourself more than a conqueror through Christ!

Now I know some of us hear this good news and think but I just wish struggle wasn't so hard. Remember Jacob. He struggled with the angel all night long before he received his blessing.

Remember Joseph. He went from the pit to the prison, and from the prison to the palace. But he had to endure enormous struggle before he arrived at the place God had for him.

Remember Moses. He struggled in Egypt trying to get the children out of Israel.

Remember Joshua. He struggled in the wilderness trying to get to the Promised Land.

Remember Daniel. He struggled in Babylon and in the lion's den.

Remember David. He struggled in the desert caves while hiding from a king who wanted him dead.

Even Jesus struggled in bringing God's dream to this earth to redeem the souls of men. He struggled in Gethsemane as He sweat great drops of blood. He struggled when He said, "Father, if it is possible, let this cup pass from me" (Matthew 26:39). He struggled when they arrested Him, mocked Him, and as He carried the cross to Calvary. But when He finally lifted His head and declared, “It is finished,” (John 19:30) the struggle was over and victory was won. God’s dream became a reality that whosoever believes in Him shall not perish but have everlasting life.

When struggle comes, consider the great cloud of witnesses who have gone before you. Hear them cheering for you from the balconies of heaven. Hear them shouting, “Press on, child of God! You are closer than you think. Press on! Hell can’t defeat you. Press on! The enemy has been defeated. Press on! The Almighty God is fighting for you. Press on! You are more than a conqueror through Christ.”

Your struggle will propel you to victory. Don’t quit on your dream because it’s gotten hard! Give God the chance to prove He can still do the impossible!

SCRIPTURE TO REMEMBER

Psalm 34:19

THINGS TO DO

Spend time remembering the great cloud of witnesses from Scripture—both the struggle they endured and the victory they won as they pressed through it. Consider what you can learn from their stories. Then re-imagine and write down how your current struggle could be propelling you forward toward your dream.

IMAGINE HOW YOUR CURRENT STRUGGLE COULD BE PROPELLING YOU TOWARDS YOUR DREAM!

THINGS TO PRAY

Ask God to help you see your current struggle from His perspective. Then thank God for providing you the strength and fortitude to press through your struggle.

CHAPTER 8

Dream Killer #6: Focusing On What Isn't

Have you ever noticed that you see what you believe you're going to see? Say you've lost your keys. You search your home and can't find them anywhere. You start again, searching in all the same places, but you don't believe the keys will be there. You look in all the usual places. No keys to be found. You look in the unusual places. Still no keys. The more you search the more the level of frustration rises within you, but still no keys. Panic begins to set in.

You're now late for an appointment. You have no idea where your keys are. How are you going to make a living without keys? You start to blame your spouse, your toddler, your roommate, your dog for hijacking your keys. Just before you sink down against the wall in abject failure and despair, you see your keys hanging on the key rack where they've been all along.

Our belief dictates our focus. Our focus dictates our reality. Another surefire way to kill your dream is to focus on what isn't. Have you ever known someone who speaks only of what they are not? They only talk of lack because their eyes only behold lack.

"Nothing good happens to me."

"I'll never make more money."

"My resume will never be good enough."

"No one will ever want to marry me."

"I'm not smart enough to write that book."

"I'll never have enough Likes on my FaceBook page."

"I'm not tall enough, funny enough, wise enough,..."

God designed and engineered you to be who you are because He is the one who planned your destiny. The quickest way to kill your dream is to talk about what's not available rather than focusing on what is. When you spend your minutes and hours pining after all that isn't, there is no capacity to find the blessings and possibilities of today. If you spend all of your energy fretting over the great job you didn't land, you can't see the dream job that's standing right in front of you. If you do nothing but wallow in your own deficit, you aren't going to see your dream become a reality.

BELIEF BECOMES REALITY

What we believe is powerful. Belief becomes focus and focus becomes reality. Even the power of God is influenced by our belief. When Jesus returned to Nazareth, the Gospel of Matthew tells us that, "He did not do many mighty works there because of their unbelief" (Matthew 13:58). Imagine that! God's work in our lives can be hampered by our own unbelief. I don't know about you, but I don't want my dream to self-destruct because I didn't really believe God is able to do what He says He will do. If you're struggling with belief, start telling yourself and the world everything that you are.

Start telling the world: "I am a child of the King of kings and Lord of lords."

"I am not powerless. I am filled with the same power that raised Jesus Christ from the grave."

"I'm not pathetic and empty—I'm filled with the abundance of El Shaddai, the all-sufficient one."

"I have a holy heritage."

"I am filled with the spiritual DNA of those who defeated giants, who crossed the sea on dry ground, who called fire from heaven, who made the dead live again."

"I feel like something good is about to happen because my God is the One who created this day, and I will rejoice and be exceedingly glad because He gave it to me."

"He filled my heart with a dream. It's not about where I am. It's not about what I'm going through. It's about what I'm going to. I'm headed to a land that is filled with milk and honey. I'm going to a place that is full of favor. I'm going to receive His goodness and His mercy. I'll declare His works in the land of the living because that's just the kind of God I serve!"

As you begin to speak this over yourself and declare it to the world, your inner person will begin to believe it. As you begin to believe it, and as you begin to focus on what is rather than what isn't, new possibilities will come alive. What looked impossible before becomes possible because God's resurrection power is at work in your life.

Remember that God didn't give you a dream to intimidate you with the impossible. He gave you a dream to show you that all things are possible. His plan is not a source of torment about what might have been. His plan is to empower you with what will be!

SCRIPTURE TO REMEMBER

Matthew 13:58
Mark 9:24

THINGS TO DO

Reflect on any areas of your life and dream where you're focusing on what isn't—whether it's something you are not or something you lack. Write those down and then write down what's true about those situations. Review what's true daily until it permeates your beliefs.

Where do you focus on what isn't?

WHAT IS TRUE ABOUT THOSE SITUATIONS?

THINGS TO PRAY

Ask God to show you where you are threatening your dream because of focusing on what isn't. Echo the cry of Mark 9:24: "Lord, I believe; help my unbelief!" and ask the Lord to help you stand firm on that which is true.

CHAPTER 9

Dream Killer #7: Unforgiveness

Have you ever thought about how seemingly unnecessary Joseph's journey was? Why was it so hard? Why did he have to end up in the pit? Why did his brothers need to plot his murder and sell him into slavery? Why the false accusations and baseless prison sentence? Surely, God Almighty could have propelled Joseph to Egypt's highest echelons another way.

But He didn't. God chose a difficult path for Joseph. God used what was intended for harm as the best path to the fulfillment of Joseph's dream. And a huge part of Joseph's success was forgiving those who pushed him down that very difficult path.

How many people do you know who are materially blessed but bankrupt inside because they won't forgive? Imagine Joseph for a moment. He's sitting in a place of enormous authority, ruling over Egypt, governing the affairs of the world. And who walks through the door? Familiar faces. There's Reuben and Judah, Levi and Simeon, Issachar, Nephtali, and Zebulun—his brothers, the sons of Jacob.

These are the men who threw him into a pit, who looked down upon him and laughed while he screamed and begged for mercy. These are the men who contrived the plan to sell him into slavery, that put him on Potiphar's floor where he was falsely accused and imprisoned, where he sat in a dungeon with tears flowing down his face, iron around his neck, and nothing but pain in his heart.

This moment is a recipe for deep hurt, anger, resentment, even hatred. As his brothers enter the palace room, Joseph recognizes them but they don't know who he is. Oh how the tables have turned! Oh what a moment for Joseph to place the same burdens on his brothers! What an opportunity to exact revenge!

Instead, in the theater of your mind, listen as Joseph begins to sob, taking off the royal Egyptian regalia, proving to his brothers that he too is a son of Jacob. Listen as he wraps his arms around them and they cry together great tears of sorrow. Listen as Joseph tells them, "You meant evil against me; but God meant it for good, in order to bring it about as it is this day, to save many people alive" (Genesis 50:20). You cursed me, but God blessed me. You sold me, but God saved me. You forgot me, but God was with me. Do you feel the redemption in this moment? Do you think it would have been possible had Joseph withheld his forgiveness for all the wrongdoing?

Because of forgiveness Joseph's dream became a reality. Because of forgiveness he was able to enjoy what God divinely planned for him. Make no mistake about it: forgiveness blesses us as much as the person we're forgiving. Maybe even more.

DIVINE FORGIVENESS

Do you wonder if forgiveness is really all that important? Consider God Almighty's dream. He wanted to redeem all the souls of men. How did He do it? Listen to Jesus' words: "Father, forgive them, for they do not know what they do" (Luke 23:34). Let the magnitude of these words settle into your heart. Even our Heavenly Father needed to forgive us in order to see His dream become a reality.

You have a choice to make today. You can look back at your past and point the finger. You can say, "If they hadn't done me wrong, I wouldn't be the way I am today." If you do, you can kiss your dream goodbye. Or, you can make the choice to believe that no matter how deep the wound, God can heal it. His plan for your life is not hindered by what others have done to you. Let me say that again: God's plan for your life is not hindered by what others have done to you. Period. If you will forgive them, your dream will soar into the future and bring with it blessings you've never known before.

SCRIPTURE TO REMEMBER

Genesis 50:20
Luke 23:34

THINGS TO DO

Ask God to show you if you're holding back forgiveness from anyone. Has someone stolen from you? Did someone stab you in the back? Were you abused? Were you mocked? Were you alone? Rejected? Make a list of those you need to forgive and bless them in Jesus' name.

WHO DO YOU NEED TO FORGIVE?

THINGS TO PRAY

Let God know who you're forgiving and releasing from past offense. It doesn't matter if you are separated by distance or death. God knows the wound and can heal it. Say: Father, I forgive them. Forgive me for holding an offense where I should have blessed them. Heal this wound within me. Amen.

SECTION 3

The Mindset of a Dreamer

CHAPTER 10

As a Man Thinks

Up to this point we've determined that today is a day for dreaming, and we've reflected on the ways that our own attitudes and actions can destroy our dreams. Now we turn to what it will take to see our dream fully realized. Do you have the mindset of a dreamer? Do you know what it takes to willingly press on when others say you should quit? If you possess a dream, you need a mindset that will guide you and protect you as your dream unfolds. The mindset of a dreamer includes:

- True belief in your dream
- To possess an attitude of excellence
- To be a doer
- To refuse to be fearful
- To capitalize on teamwork, and
- To live a balanced life.

As we delve into the mindset of a dreamer, ask God to speak to you about your dream and the steps you need to take to make it a reality.

I have a friend who dreamed of building the finest vineyard in the State of Texas. He spent four years attending seminars, interviewing viticulturalists, educating himself on varietals and pruning techniques, and creating a maze of financial projections. What can I say? My friend needed a hobby.

Today, eight years later, there is a beautiful vineyard growing on the High Plains just outside of Lubbock. What's interesting to me is that what is visible only now, eight years later, is what this man saw from the very beginning. Because he truly believed in his dream, he knew what it was going to look like long before it ever became a reality.

What we believe about our dream will make or break its success. There's just no way of getting around this. Proverbs 23:7 says, "For as [a person] thinks in his heart, so is he." As we really believe, as we really think, so we are. If you want your dream to become a reality, you need to believe in it with all of your being, and you need to believe God is able to do the impossible, regardless of your circumstances.

What does it mean to believe in your dream? It means you know and absorb your dream fully, and you believe in its success. Dreamers believe their dream will come true before their eyes ever see it unfold. They even know in large part what will unfold. Edison knew the light bulb would dispel darkness before one was ever created. Orville and Wilbur Wright knew it was possible to fly before they ever built Kitty Hawk. Alexander Graham Bell knew it was possible to improve the speed of communication before he invented the telephone.

When you know your dream, you so inhabit the depths of it that you know what its tiniest details are. Remember the expression "I want it so bad I can taste it"? When you believe in your dream down to your core, you inhabit it so fully you will even know its taste.

WRITE IT DOWN

The most powerful way to fully inhabit your dream is to follow the prophet Habakkuk's advice: "Write the vision and make it plain on tablets, that he may run who reads it" (Habakkuk 2:2). That's exactly what you have been doing throughout this journal—writing things down and making them plain. Sound unimpressive?

There's a very godly, very wealthy man who lives

in the South. Long before he ever became wealthy he inhabited his dream and absorbed it fully. He thought long and hard about exactly what his dream was. Then, on a stack of notecards, he wrote down the details of that dream: where he would live when his dream became a reality, what the make, model, and color of his car would be, even the number he would see in his bank account. Each day, as he was driving to and from work, he reviewed those notecards and vividly imagined each detail in his mind until they were completely absorbed into his belief system.

Do you know in five years time his life was an exact reflection of those notecards? Today he owns companies you would readily recognize and it all began with inhabiting his dream, writing down its details on inexpensive notecards, and absorbing each and every one.

Don't underestimate the power of writing your dream down plainly. If you cannot write down in simple words what you want to happen, then you don't really know what it is that you want to happen. If that is the case for you, spend time reflecting on what it is. If you don't know what you want, it's highly unlikely you'll ever achieve your God-given dream.

BEHOLD YOUR DREAM

Once you can articulate your dream fully, the next step is to absorb it. Think about what the Bible says. Throughout scripture, chapter after chapter, we are told "keep this in front of your eyes," "keep this in your heart," "keep this in your mouth." Why? Because we become what we behold. As a man thinks, so he is.

If you write down your dream, and you put that piece of paper in a place where you will see it on a regular basis, and you behold that dream over and over, you will become that dream. Think about it. If you pick up a newspaper and behold the headlines of fear and scarcity, you will become the headlines, believing in and seeing fear and scarcity. If you read the things of this world and absorb them, you will be on a course to become what the world says you will be. But if you read the things of God and absorb them, then you will become the head and not the tail, above only and not beneath, blessed in the city, blessed in the field, and blessed in whatever you do.

This is something that will change your life, the life of your children, and the life of your children's children. Truly believe in your dream. Inhabit it fully. Write it down plainly. Behold it often and absorb it completely. Believe in faith that God will bring this great thing to fruition, and then watch expectantly for it!

SCRIPTURE TO REMEMBER

Proverbs 23:7
Habakkuk 2:2

THINGS TO DO

In Section 1 we started with a more general dream. If you haven't already, now is the time to start filling in the specifics of your dream. Start imagining the details of your dream. Write them down plainly. Keep these details in a place you will see often. Sometimes it's your bathroom mirror; sometimes it's the console of your vehicle; or it can be this dream journal. Behold your dream frequently and absorb it fully. If you don't yet know your dream, continue asking God to reveal it to you. Don't give up! Believe that He will answer you.

GET SPECIFIC! WRITE DOWN THE DETAILS OF YOUR DREAM.

Get specific! Write down the details of your dream. continued

THINGS TO PRAY

Ask the Lord to help you take Him at His Word so you can fully believe in your dream even to the smallest detail. Say: I believe anything is possible with You and I believe in faith that You will bring this dream to fruition.

CHAPTER 11

An Attitude of Excellence

In addition to truly believing in your dream, the mindset of a dreamer also includes an attitude of excellence. You need to know there is a difference between your capability, your motivation, and your attitude. Capability describes your power—what you have the ability to do. Motivation is why you do what you do. And attitude has everything to do with how well you do what you do.

On a Saturday evening in any city there are hundreds of waiters ready to serve customers a meal. A waiter is capable of taking an order. He is capable of handing that order to the chef. And the motivation for his service is the promise of a tip after the meal. But if he waits on a table and has a bad attitude, how large will his tip be? Sometimes we walk into a restaurant and see someone who possesses reasonable capability and motivation, but their poor attitude makes for dismal results. The world is full of people with bad attitudes. But if you're going to be a dreamer you can't be one of them. You've got to have an attitude of excellence.

What defines an attitude of excellence? An attitude of excellence is always thinking about what you have to do to get where you want to go. It's not stuck on what offense happened this morning or the bad night's sleep you had last night. Consider Joseph again. He did not allow his circumstances to define him. Through excellence he changed his circumstances. Joseph had a dream he was going to rule. But before God gave him authority to rule over anyone else, he first had to rule over himself. He saw himself ruling over Egypt, but had he not been able to control himself, God wouldn't have handed him a nation.

EXCELLENCE IN THE SMALL THINGS

The Bible says, "Well done, good and faithful servant; you were faithful over a few things, I will make you ruler over many things...." (Matthew 25:21). Why would God allow you to lead others if you can't lead yourself? Why would God bring your dream to fulfillment if you can't handle it yet? The first person to ever sit in submission to Joseph was Joseph. And it was there that he practiced an attitude of excellence.

He ruled over himself with an attitude of excellence when he scrubbed Potiphar's floor. Was that where he wanted to be? No. But because he did it well, he was promoted. He ruled over himself when Potiphar's wife tempted him. He ruled over himself when he went to prison. He ruled over himself when they appointed him trustee. He ruled over himself the day he came out of the dungeon and sat in diadems—all because he had an attitude of excellence. Each step of his journey, he behaved as if he believed his dream was going to come true. And you know what? "The Lord was with Joseph, and he was a successful man" (Genesis 39:2).

Joseph behaved as if he believed his dream would come true, and the Lord was with Joseph. You need to know his brothers forsook him, but God was with him. Potiphar abused him, but God was with him. Others falsely accused him, but God was with him. His fellow prisoners forgot him, but God was with him. The world can put you through hell and back, but if God is with you victory is within reach!

EXCELLENCE ALWAYS PERSEVERES

In addition to always thinking about where you're headed, an attitude of excellence always perseveres. Struggle is ever before us but an attitude of excellence believes that God has a better tomorrow in your future. The Apostle Paul had this attitude when he said, "Brethren, I do not count myself to have apprehended; but one thing I do, forgetting those things which are behind and reaching forward to those things which are ahead" (Philippians 3:13).

He reached forward to a goal—the goal of a divine dream that God planted in his heart. Paul made up his mind that no matter what it took, he was going to press through the pain of his past, he was going to press through the trials of today, he was going to press through the rejection of others, he was going to press through the fears he was facing—he was going to persevere through it all with an attitude of excellence because God had something better for him. And in so doing, he announced to the world, the flesh, and the devil that he could do all things through Christ who gave him strength (see Philippians 4:13).

You've got to refuse to let current circumstances destroy your dream. An attitude of excellence does not whine about where you are today. It doesn't worry about what you are not or what you cannot do. An attitude of excellence doesn't mock your today—it celebrates the opportunity to rule over yourself. An attitude of excellence is always thinking about what you have to do to get where you want to go and persevering through every obstacle. Follow in Joseph's footsteps. Don't allow circumstances to define you. Through excellence, change your circumstances. You can do this, child of God! Press on!

SCRIPTURE TO REMEMBER

Matthew 25:21
Genesis 39:2
Philippians 3:13
Philippians 4:13

THINGS TO DO

Reflect on your attitude. Do you possess an attitude of excellence? Are there any areas where you need to better focus on your dream? Are there any obstacles or circumstances you need perseverance to overcome? List these out and determine how you will respond with an attitude of excellence.

Do you possess an attitude of excellence? Why or why not?

How can you better focus on your dream?

What circumstances or obstacles do you need to overcome?

How will you respond with an attitude of excellence?

THINGS TO PRAY

Confess to God any area where your attitude has not been like Joseph's or Paul's. Ask God to help you know His nearness as you persevere.

CHAPTER 12

Dreamers Are Doers

Have you ever wanted to lose a few pounds? Did you lose those pounds by wishing really hard? Did you do so by sitting on the couch watching workout videos? How about laying waste to an extra large supreme pizza—did that help? I'm guessing not. Whether your dream is one of health, home, or career, your dream will not work until you do.

Dreamers not only believe in their dreams and possess an attitude of excellence, dreamers are doers. If you have the mindset of a dreamer, you've got to do. The difference between what you wish for and what you receive is what you're willing to do about it. We all wish for things, but only those who are willing to do something about it see their wishes fulfilled. Lots of people want to be an Olympian and win the gold medal. But do you know how many will receive it? One. And I'll bet that champion did more than any of the other competitors for that gold medal. When you're willing to do what others will not, you'll go beyond everyone else. You can't just dream about some grand outcome, you've got to do something about it. Dreamers are doers.

THE FUEL OF OUR FAITH

The Bible says it this way, "Faith without works is dead" (James 2:26). Now let me clarify: I didn't say faith is powerless. Faith is powerful. So much so that Jesus said if we would only have faith the size of a mustard seed we could move mountains (Matthew 17:20). Faith is powerful but the fuel of faith is our effort. If we're not willing to work at faith, faith will not work in us. We can't just dream about something; we've got to put forth effort to make it a reality.

Some people dream about having a great marriage. But again, you can't just wish for it, you've got to do the work. You have to invest your life in the life of your spouse so that your marriage is extraordinary. You can't simply dictate your demands of what your partner needs to change to please you. I imagine both spouses involved could create impressive lists of what the other one needed to change. If you want an outstanding marriage you have to be the kind of spouse you're dreaming of. As you love your spouse the way you wish to be loved, watch and see if your spouse's behavior doesn't become more loving to you.

In 1 Peter, Peter is speaking to women who have come to faith in Christ though their spouses haven't. These women are righteous; their husbands are not. Peter doesn't tell them to go home and write a note that says, "In case of rapture, read this." And he doesn't tell them to leave notes all over the house that say, "You're going to hell!" No, of course Peter isn't going to say that.

During the first century in the Middle East, women were property, not human beings. If someone had a daughter and there was a man who wanted to marry her, her father traded her for livestock, land, or riches. That's not how you treat people; that's how you treat property. Husbands could divorce their wives without cause or ramification.

In this very delicate cultural circumstance, Peter says to these women: Go live your life in such a way that without a word your wicked husbands will observe your godly conduct and themselves want to become godly. It was all about the actions of these women that fueled their faith for the salvation of each of their husbands.

Look at it this way. If, God forbid, I pass before my wife, I want my wife to walk next to another man and speak of nothing but me because his love for her cannot begin to compare to how lavishly I loved her. "When Matt brought me here he gave me the most beautiful flowers." "When Matt brought me here, he took care of such and such." "When Matt did this... When Matt did this... When Matt did this..." This poor other man will meet me in heaven one day and I'll be grinning from ear to ear because I made his life miserable. How? By doing.

If you want a great marriage, if you want to be fit, if you want to earn a PhD, if you want to write your magnum opus—folks, you can't just wish upon a star. You have to do the work. You say, "I'm dreaming of a great business." That's nice but you have to make a great business! You say, "But preacher, conditions are tough." Well then, you get tougher! Plan A didn't work, then try again. You say, "Oh but it's not going the way I thought it would." Then adapt! You need to change something around, find a new way forward. Business takes effort. Marriage takes effort. Dreams take effort. There's a Latin phrase *solvitur ambulando* that means: "It is solved by walking." Friends, dreams come true by walking it out, by doing, by adapting, and by working.

THE EXTRA MILE

Now when you start working on your dream, decide what kind of work you're going to do. Jesus told His disciples, "Whoever compels you to go one mile, go with him two" (Matthew 5:41). The work we're talking about here is not what is merely required. The work of dreams is to do more than what is required.

Declare war on average and mediocre. Refuse to be anything less than your absolute best. That's how you plan on success: you always go that extra mile. You want to be a football champion? Have more discipline than everyone else. You want to be a world-class artist? Practice longer than everyone else. Want to move people with words? There are no short cuts, you must put in the effort.

ONE THING EVERY DAY

Now go back in this journal and look at your dream. Right now, make a conscious decision that each and every day you will do at least one thing that will bring you closer to your dream. You can always do more than that, but do at least one. If you do just one thing every day, and string enough 'one day's' together, the next thing you know you've made what we call progress. You're not going to achieve your dream overnight. But you will see your dream become reality if only you don't give up!

Here's the thing: It's God who ultimately brings you wealth (see Deuteronomy 8:18). If you put God first, if you seek His kingdom and His righteousness, He will add everything else to you (see Matthew 6:33). He will do the miraculous things you cannot. And if you are working toward your goal every day, and if God is on your side, the one thing you cannot do is fail. So do not be afraid. Put your faith in God, get to work, prime the well, and let the blessings of heaven fall!

SCRIPTURE TO REMEMBER

James 2:26
Matthew 17:20
Deuteronomy 8:18
Matthew 6:33
Matthew 5:41

THINGS TO DO

Make a list of actions you can take to bring you closer to your dream. Break them into small tasks that can be done throughout the year. Track your progress. Ask someone you trust to hold you accountable to completing the tasks that help you make progress.

What actions will make your dream a reality?

List daily tasks that will bring you closer to your dream

January

February

List daily tasks that will bring you closer to your dream

March

April

List daily tasks that will bring you closer to your dream

May

June

LIST DAILY TASKS THAT WILL BRING YOU CLOSER TO YOUR DREAM

JULY

AUGUST

List daily tasks that will bring you closer to your dream

September

October

List daily tasks that will bring you closer to your dream

November

December

THINGS TO PRAY

Ask God to fuel your effort and grant you wisdom in creating a sound strategy. Ask Him for courage on days that you're fearful, encouragement on days when you're discouraged, and energy on days when you're weary.

CHAPTER 13

DREAMERS REFUSE TO BE FEARFUL

As a kid, were you ever scared of the dark? Did you ever have one of those nights where you thought you heard something in your closet and you froze stone solid under your blanket? That kind of fear paralyzes you completely. Even if you wanted to move, your body wouldn't let you. Fear can do the same thing to a dreamer just as it can to a young child in the dark.

The mindset of a dreamer, however, refuses to be fearful. I want to be very clear from the start about the difference between having fears and being fearful. When you have fear, you're a human being. There are studies that show us that fear is actually a helpful part of our lives. Fear is a gift that helps us know when something isn't right, when we should be cautious, or when we should refuse that ride home with a stranger offering candy. But when you're fearful, fear paralyzes you. It causes you to freeze when what you need to do is move forward.

Some of you may say, "Well, I just don't allow fear into my life."

Well then, you're a better person than the rest of us. Even giant-killing King David wrote, "I sought the Lord, and He heard me, and delivered me from all my fears" (Psalm 34:4). If he was courageous and still had fear, then you need to know you'll have fears too. The mindset of a dreamer allows God to deliver us from our fears rather than allow fear to hold us hostage.

MOSES AND FEAR

Let's look at Moses' story. The Egyptians have held the Israelites as slaves for many years. After the plagues fall upon Egypt, Pharaoh relents, releases the Israelites, and Moses leads them out—still very aware that they remain in grave danger. There's a moment on their journey out of Egypt when Moses sees the great Red Sea in front of them and knows that Pharaoh is right on their heels. He looks up to heaven as if to say, "Hey! Are you paying attention? We've got the sea before us and an angry army behind us!"

And God says to Moses: "'Do not be afraid. Stand

still, and see the salvation of the Lord, which He will accomplish for you today. For the Egyptians whom you see today, you shall see again no more forever'" (Exodus 14:13). That's quite a revelation.

So after this tremendous conversation with God what does Moses do? He turns slowly around to the people of Israel. He stares into their frightened eyes and tries to calm his breathing as Pharaoh's army rapidly approaches... and he begins to speak. He holds up his staff dramatically and says in his best stage voice, "Behold Israel, this Pharaoh that you see before you, you shall see no more."

But before he can continue, God interrupts him. "'Why do you cry out to Me? Tell the children of Israel to go forward'" (Exodus 14:15). God is saying: "I'm not impressed with your poetry, Moses. I told you I was going to get you out of this. If you will stop flapping your gums and get in the water, I can do something that will change the world."

Why was Moses standing around pontificating to the children of Israel? Because while he's looking and speaking in their direction, he's peeking over his shoulder at the water.

He's wondering: Is anything happening out there?

But he's saying, "Behold, O Israel, God is going to do great things!"

He's thinking: Do you hear me, God?

And God stops him to say, "Quit being so afraid! I told you what I was going to do. Now I need you to move forward so that I can do it. Stop standing on the banks staring at your problem. Walk towards it and see if I will not make a way where there seems to be no way!"

There was a moment when Moses had a choice to look fear full in the face and move forward, or to let fear paralyze him. Moses made a choice in that moment to allow God to deliver him—and the entire nation of Israel—from fear rather than succumb to it.

FEAR OF MAKING A MISTAKE

One of the things people are most afraid of is making a mistake. "Well I'd do something," we hear, "but I'm just afraid I'm going to mess it up." Let me give you this assurance today: You will make a mistake. Everyone does!

When you make a mistake, take responsibility for it and then move forward. If you didn't do it right, go back and fix it. If you can't fix it, find someone who can help you fix it. And then get over it and move forward.

How many of our lives get hijacked because we park by a mistake? Imagine if Moses had said to God, "I think I heard you say we should wade into that water but what if I'm wrong? This is too big a decision to mess up so I'm going to sit this one out." Pharaoh's army would have destroyed the Israelites!

Friends, when you make a mistake declare that because God is with you that He can use all things for your good and for His glory. Know that your mistake is not bigger than God's redemption.

Winston Churchill, one of the greatest leaders of all time, said, "The price of greatness is responsibility." You want to be great? Be responsible. And don't just be responsible for what goes right. Be responsible for what goes right and what goes wrong. Have you ever met the guy who's in charge of everything good?

The company president says, "I'm proud of how our company achieved this milestone."

Mr. In-Charge-of-Everything-Good says, "Oh, I did that!"

The company president says, "I didn't like how our company fell flat on this objective."

And Mr. In-Charge-of-Everything-Good says, "Oh, I had nothing to do that. That was all them, not me!"

Responsibility goes both ways. In fact, the most valuable people to any institution are those who can fix mistakes, not those who take credit for things that are already working.

Mistakes are part of our journey. Take responsibility for yours, declare that God can use them, and keep moving forward!

WRITE DOWN YOUR FEARS

The power of writing down your dreams is equally as valuable for your fears too. You know your dream is something you will take action on. Likewise your fears are something you will face. In fact, the only way fears are conquered is when you face them. Fear cannot be ignored. It will hover close and tap, tap, tap on your shoulder. You cannot run from fear. If you do, once you stop to take a breath, fear will be staring you in the face. But if you will face fear, it will disappear.

How do you do that? Write down your fears in this journal and call it your Hit List. Start thinking about how you're going to take these fears out of your life. Once you've listed out your fears, write a battle plan for how you're going to conquer each fear so it stays in your past and doesn't haunt your future.

Here's an example. Let's say you fear criticism. You're afraid to move forward in your dream because it might draw critics. Listen, if you're not being criticized you're not trying hard enough! If your dream doesn't bring criticism, then it's not worth dreaming.

On your Hit List, your battle plan for fear of criticism could be to actively rejoice and offer thanksgiving each time you receive criticism. If you have the heart and mindset of a dreamer, every time someone begins to criticize you, look at your critic as if they're throwing you a pep rally on the way to your destiny. Criticism ought to be the battle hymn of every true dreamer that's ever lived! If they don't use words like "crazy," then you're not dreaming big enough! If you hear, "That'll never happen!" respond with a resounding, "Yes! Then it's bound to succeed!"

Maybe you're afraid because no one else has ever accomplished what it is you wish to accomplish. I assure you, when the pain of giving up your dream outweighs your fear of failure, you will ignore failure and press on!

Maybe you're afraid because your dream will cost you something. Folks, if your dream isn't costing you something, then it's not worth having.

Whatever your fears are, write them down on your Hit List and then plan to face and conquer them. Regardless of what they are, don't allow your fears to freeze you. Achievement only comes through action. And if you're going to take action, you've got to face your fears.

If you have allowed fear to stop you mid-step, hear the Word of God say to you today: Move forward! Move forward toward that mountain and see if God won't cast it into the midst of the sea. Move forward toward that giant and see if he doesn't get smaller with every step that you take. Move forward into that valley and see if the Light of the world will not walk through the darkest valley with you. Move forward and declare with every step that you take: God has not given me a spirit of fear, but one of power, and one of love, and one of sound mind. And because God is with me, who can stand against me? I'm more than a conqueror through Christ!

SCRIPTURE TO REMEMBER

Psalm 34:4
Exodus 14:13–15

THINGS TO DO

Think about any fears that keep you from pursuing your dream. Create a Hit List and your battle plan for facing those fears. Declare that God has not given you a spirit of fear, but one of power, and one of love, and one of sound mind. Because God is with you, who can stand against you? You are more than a conqueror through Christ!

What is your hit list?

WHAT IS YOUR BATTLE PLAN FOR DEFEATING YOUR HIT LIST?

THINGS TO PRAY

Thank God for delivering you from your fears. Ask Him to show you any fears that are holding you back from pursuing your dream. Pray for the courage to face those fears head on and to keep moving forward.

CHAPTER 14

Teamwork Makes the Dream Work

Dreamers believe in their dreams, they're doers, they refuse to be fearful, and—very importantly—dreamers understand that teamwork makes the dream work. I don't care who you are, no one accomplishes a dream on their own.

Look at Cornerstone Church. Do you know what it takes for this church to function? Teamwork. Sure, you see a pastor up front and can assume it's all because of that person's efforts. But there isn't any one person at Cornerstone who accomplishes its work on his or her own.

You say, "Well, I'm going to church to hear the pastor."

Fantastic. I'm so glad you did! But you know who else I'm glad for? The folks who take care of the restrooms each weekend before anyone arrives to hear the sermon. Everybody has a role. Everybody has a place. Everybody has a purpose.

WE NEED EACH OTHER

If you think you can do your dream by your own lonesome, you'd be the very first one that ever could. When God created a perfect earth He created Adam and placed him in it. He looked at Adam and said, "It is not good that man should be alone; I will make him a helper comparable to him" (Genesis 2:18). The boy didn't even have a chance to mess up and God didn't let him go at it all by himself! Why? Because no one can do it on his or her own.

We're designed to compliment each other. We're designed to need each other. God made us to be relational. My strengths compliment your weaknesses. Your strengths compliment my weaknesses. That's why the Bible says, "Though one may be overpowered by another, two can withstand him. And a threefold cord is not quickly broken" (Ecclesiastes 4:12).

When my strengths and your strengths get together, we cancel out our weaknesses and now we are complete. Teamwork makes the dream work. Kendal and I use this statement in our home all the time. Why?

Because she and I have very difference strengths. She's an ICU nurse. She looks at details. She looks at monitors and heartbeats and all these different little things to assess how a patient is doing. I'm a big picture guy. If I were to assess a patient, I would only check to see if they're breathing! I plan at a 30,000-foot perspective: Let's host our family for Christmas dinner! Kendal plans at the 30-foot perspective: how to logistically feed an army going ninety miles a minute. We need each other. Teamwork makes our dream work because together we're complete.

TRUST

In order for teamwork to happen, you have to trust the people on your team. In fact, if you don't trust them to do their job, then you're not a good member of your own team. If a pastor decided the folks cleaning the church restrooms didn't do their job well, and spent the entire week cleaning each stall and mirror and replacing all that toilet paper, how would a sermon be written? How would counseling happen? How would a marriage be officiated and a new widow comforted? If you spend your waking moments micromanaging your team, you won't have enough time to do your part of the dream.

Think about the people who surround you. God wrote a cast of characters into your life very specifically and purposefully. All of your friends, all of your foes—no one showed up on accident. When he designed you, he appointed them to you. The people you like, God gave them to you. The people you don't like, God gave them to you too. Sometimes an adversary can take you farther than an ally. Who really set up David's career? It wasn't Saul or Jonathan. It was Goliath. David was anointed to be King. But standing out there in the shepherd fields he was just one of the boys. When he stood in front of that giant, that's when he became the man.

Understand that every set of helping hands, every voice of encouragement, every word of wisdom, none of it goes wasted in God's kingdom—because teamwork makes the dream work, and the only way to make a team work is to trust your team. Stop thinking you can do this dream on your own. And start trusting the people God purposefully put in your path to do their part.

TEAMWORK IN MOSES' LIFE

Moses understood the power of teamwork when he delegated authority to a trusted group of men in the book of Exodus. He was wearing himself out believing it was his sole responsibility to care for the entire nation of Israel. Imagine that pressure!

His father-in-law watched him act as judge for the Israelites from morning until night and said to him, "[This] thing that you do is not good. Both you and these people who are with you will surely wear yourselves out. For this thing is too much for you; you are not able to perform it by yourself" (Exodus 18:18). And then he tells Moses to select men who are willing and able to help him lead the Israelites (see Exodus 18:21–23).

In your own life, as you consider those who surround you, select your teammates based on solid qualifications: they need to be willing and able. My sons are willing to help me build a house, but they're not yet able to. Some people are willing but not able. Others are able but not willing. When the two come together, you've got a teammate you can trust.

TEAMWORK IN JESUS' LIFE

Even God chose a team to fulfill His dream. Did Jesus complete a solo journey for the redemption of humanity? No. Jesus delegated authority to the New Testament church. He selected men who were willing and able to be His disciples. For three years He trained them. He laid His hands on them. He empowered them with His Spirit. He sent them out, saying, "Go into all the world and preach the gospel to every creature" (Mark 16:15). And what did those men do? They turned the world upside down!

The disciples didn't allow their fear to paralyze them. They weren't waiting for God to give them detailed orders each day. Because God delegated His authority, they cast out demons and laid hands on the sick. What they asked for in faith, God did. And the world was forever changed because they were willing to live out the dream God placed in their hearts. Teamwork makes the dream work. It was true for God Almighty and it's true for you and for me.

Some of you aren't yet dreaming. Some of you are dreaming alone. Some of you are trying to do it on your own. And before your dream becomes a reality, you need to know that God has placed people in your path you can and should trust to help you accomplish what He's given you to do. Choose your teammates wisely and watch how the Lord will bring your dream to reality through the work of many hands.

SCRIPTURE TO REMEMBER

Genesis 2:18
Ecclesiastes 4:12
Exodus 18:18–23
Mark 16:15

THINGS TO DO

Consider the people in your life. Who would make a good teammate for you as you pursue your dream? Who has proven themselves to be willing and able? Write those names down and pray over them. When the season is right, discuss your dream with each one and invite their participation as appropriate. Remember, each must be willing and able. Respect any No's you receive as much as the Yes's.

Who do you want on your team? Why?

THINGS TO PRAY

Thank God for the teammates He's already placed in your life and ask for discernment and wisdom in selecting teammates in the future. Ask the Lord to help build trust throughout your team, and multiply your efforts as He makes your dream a reality.

CHAPTER 15

DREAMERS LIVE A LIFE OF BALANCE

Have you ever witnessed someone so focused on a goal that they ended up destroying themselves in the pursuit of that goal? Athletes can do this. An athlete can train so long and so hard for competition that his body breaks under the constant pressure, and he has to forfeit his chance to compete. Folks, without balance, the same thing can happen to us as we pursue our dream. If we do nothing but pursue our dream to the detriment of our family, our walk with God, our health—then the very thing we're after will be the very thing that takes us out.

When you have the mindset of a dreamer, you recognize that dreamers live a life of balance. Dreamers are not so heavenly minded that they're no earthly good. You're dreaming about great things? That's fabulous. Go to work. Dream about tomorrow but live in the balance of today. If your dream for a successful business is going to become a reality, you've got to be able to balance both the business and your family. You've got to be able to balance your work and your worship. You've got to be able to balance all of the areas of your life so you don't get out of balance and destroy yourself pursuing your dream.

Solomon addresses this when he says, "Do not be overly righteous, nor be overly wise: why should you destroy yourself?" (Ecclesiastes 7:16). When you are out of balance, even good things can destroy you. The mindset of a dreamer recognizes that you can be too focused on a great dream. Don't neglect to care for your family and yourself while you're building the next great widget. You've got to balance your expectations of what will be with your accomplishments of what already is. Yes, you expect greater things tomorrow, but you understand that you've got to work in order to accomplish for today.

REALITY CHECK

Dreamers have a realistic perspective of who they are and where they're at. They don't start leading a Bible study of five and call themselves "Bishop." That's not dreaming—that's delusional. But when they start leading that Bible study, they lead it as well as they can because to those who are faithful over a few things, God will give more. They understand that doing their very best today gives them permission to be promoted tomorrow.

You say, "But preacher, you don't understand. My boss is out control. She expects me to do the work of three different people. How can I stick with this job and pursue my dream?" Look at it this way: All those different jobs you're doing, all those different contacts you're making, all those various industries you're venturing into—all of those pieces may be exactly what you need in order to move into the next phase of your dream. If you stick with it, you just might discover that all this work today is the experience you need for your dream job tomorrow.

Be realistic about what is before you today. Be faithful to the obligations in front of you. The moments of your today will bring you to the dream of your tomorrow.

You need to know, too, that sometimes the reality check for a life of balance is a wakeup call. For some of us we pursue our dream to the detriment of our lives. And for others of us we pursue our lives to the detriment of our dream. If there isn't room in your life to pursue your dream, something is out of balance. If you keep putting off your dream until the kids are in school or until you have the perfect art studio or until you land the corner office, more than likely you'll never get around to working on it. For dreamers, a life of balance ensures they make time to pursue their dream.

THE DREAM PICKED YOU

Whether you know it or not, you didn't pick your dream. Your dream picked you. If your dream came from the heart of God, then He designed you to live it out. Remember God's dream of redeeming the world? Jesus told His disciples, "You did not choose Me, but I chose you and appointed you that you should go and bear fruit, and that your fruit should remain, that whatever you ask the Father in My name He may give you" (John 15:16). The disciples didn't choose this dream. Jesus chose each of them.

When Jesus said these words the disciples were dreaming. They were dreaming that in just a few hours, they were going to be a part of the millennial kingdom. They were dreaming that in just a few days people were going to revere them because they were so faithful to Jesus. And Jesus said, "Your heads are in the clouds, but I need your feet down here on earth. I picked you to produce fruit. Now go to work."

Dreamers live a life of balance because they know their dream is part of their destiny. Your dream works in tandem with your family. Your dream works in tandem with your health. God isn't going to bless you with twelve kids and then tell you to abandon them to pursue your dream. Your kids will impact you in ways that shape your dream. If you're single, your friends and extended family will impact you in ways that shape your dream. Don't abandon your community because you have a dream. When your dream is part of your destiny, every person in your life, every experience, every failure, every success, it all works together for God's glory. Your responsibility is to live with balance.

Are you living a life of balance today? Have you put your life on hold to pursue your dream? Are you neglecting your life in order to pursue your dream? Have you made room in your life to pursue a dream? Dreamers fully expect that one day they will achieve what they're dreaming about, but they do not allow that passion to make them impatient and run past the moments of today. When you have the mindset of a dreamer, you accept where you were and you continue to push through the obstacles of your present in order to get where you want to go. Yes, dream big. But do the work of today. Stay engaged in the present. And rest in the knowledge that God will be faithful to bring about your dream in His perfect timing.

SCRIPTURE TO REMEMBER

Ecclesiastes 7:16
John 15:16

THINGS TO DO

Reflect on your life. Write down any areas that are out of balance. Then determine how you will make changes to your daily rhythm to restore balance. Because change is part of our everyday existence, living a balanced life will take continual effort. Commit to making it a priority for you and your family. Check in with yourself and with your spouse on a regular basis to reevaluate when additional changes need to be made.

What areas of your life are out of balance?

WHAT CHANGES CAN YOU MAKE TO RESTORE BALANCE?

THINGS TO PRAY

You are the God of order and balance. You are the God who worked for six days and rested on the seventh. Help me live likewise. Open my heart to any place that is out of balance and help me restore it. And help me rest in who You are, knowing that You will ultimately bring my dream to fruition.

CONCLUSION

Do we dare to dream? Do we dare to pursue our divine destiny? It's a lot of work, faith, trust, hope, and patience. And I know there are times when we wonder if all that we've just discussed really works. Does any of it—daring to dream, guarding against the dream killers, writing your dreams and fears down, possessing the mindset of a dreamer— really make a difference?

Folks, I know for a fact it does. Hanging on Pastor Hagee's office wall is the back cover of a Bible that he used back in the early 90s. He was at a convention over two decades ago when he began writing down his dreams for Cornerstone Church. He wrote that one day Cornerstone Church would have a television ministry that would reach the nations of the world. As of 2015, there are more than a hundred nations watching what's happening in San Antonio, Texas because of the television ministry.

Pastor Hagee wrote on the back cover of his Bible that Cornerstone Church would have a conference center with a campground. And that the campground would be a place where people would receive training, ministry, and deliverance. That place is called Tarpley, Texas. And it's about an hour outside of San Antonio.

He wrote down that Cornerstone Church would have a school. And that the school would be a place to raise up godly children with a Christ-centered education. He wrote that vision long before Cornerstone Christian Schools became a reality in 1993. In 2015 we began working on a new campus site where the school will relocate to.

Pastor Hagee wrote each of these dreams down just as Habakkuk 2 instructs. He laid these dreams before the Lord and God fulfilled every single one of them. Why? Because God gives us the desires of our heart. Dreams really do come true.

The Sovereign God, the One who sees the end from the beginning, has you in one hand and your destiny in another. If you'll put your faith in Him, He will move heaven and earth to bring the two together. God is pulling you toward a destiny that He designed for you before the world began. You just have to be willing to put your faith in His Word, to stand upon His promises, to do the work before you, and to let Him prove that He is able to do the impossible.

God says in Isaiah, "[My Word] shall not return to Me void, but it shall accomplish what I please, and it shall prosper in the thing for which I sent it" (55:11). Trust in Him and not your own understanding and you will see your dream become a reality!

Dare to Dream!

Dare to Dream!

Dare to Dream!

Dare to Dream!

Dare to Dream!

Dare to Dream!

Dare to Dream!

Dare to Dream!

Dare to Dream!

Dare to Dream!

Dare to Dream!

Dare to Dream!

Dare to Dream!

Dare to Dream!

Dare to Dream!

Dare to Dream!

Dare to Dream!

Dare to Dream!

Dare to Dream!

Dare to Dream!

Dare to Dream!

Dare to Dream!

Dare to Dream!